T0167303

Set Free

How God Rescues Us from Lives of Shame, Guilt, & Sin

Harrison Glenn Prins

Order this book online at www.trafford.com
or email orders@trafford.com

Most Trafford titles are also available at major online book retailers.

Printed in Victoria, BC, Canada.

ISBN: 978-1-4269-2865-9 (sc)
ISBN: 978-1-4269-3240-3 (eb)

Library of Congress Control Number: 2010903510

*Our mission is to efficiently provide the world's finest, most comprehensive
book publishing service, enabling every author to experience success.
To find out how to publish your book, your way, and have it available
worldwide, visit us online at www.trafford.com*

Trafford rev. 04/23/2010

 www.trafford.com

North America & international
toll-free: 1 888 232 4444 (USA & Canada)
phone: 250 383 6864 ♦ fax: 812 355 4082

Dedication

This book is dedicated to a number of wonderful people in my life: people who have taught me some valuable lessons and who have showed me that God's love is all I need to move on in my life.

- To my musical inspiration: Mrs. Sandi Patti Helvering Peslis. Thanks Sandi for teaching all of us to use our gifts for Christ, for blessing us with your 3+ decades of music, and for being an example of what redemption looks like.

- To my therapist and friend: Mrs. Toni Jauregui. Thanks "Tone" for our weekly talks and for helping me grow spiritually and socially. I also thank you for helping me overcome some of the social obstacles that come with

Asperger Syndrome. You truly are an angel in human form.

- To my dear friend and mentor: Pastor Will Verhoef. Thanks "Willie" for all the lunch talks and hugs, the bright smiles, and your compassion and caring heart. You and Ruth have blessed my life beyond my wildest dreams.

- To my youth minister: Mr. Nick In't Hout. Thanks "Nicky" for all of your encouraging words, and the ability to work with you on those SERVE projects over the last several years. Your confidence has helped me shoot for my dreams.

- To my dear friend and fellow songwriter: Mr. Jeffrey Mercer. Thanks "Jeffy" for the hugs, the time spent at the piano putting my lyrics to music, your countless hours of rewriting my songs (I mean our songs), and your Godly example. I don't know how I could have made it through 2009 without you and your help.

- To the "J" family, the Smiths, the Harry Prins, Jr. family, the Wagners, Uncle Mike and the Michiganders, and the Doug Jorritsma family.

Thanks for helping me realize God's plan for my life, being a great Godly support system, and for just being you.

- To my grandparents: Mr. George and Mrs. Marvalee Johnson Jorritsma, and Mr. Harry Prins, Sr. and Mrs. Lois Zuidema Prins. Thanks for showing a Godly example for over 50 years. Blessings like that don't happen overnight, and I pray that the Lord allows me to meet someone special and remain married to her for at least that long. Also, thank you for being there in the bad times and good, helping whenever and wherever possible.

- To Mitchell, Cameron, and Clara. Thanks guys for being the greatest siblings any guy could ask for. I love you all deeply and am glad that I could be part of your lives for 18 years. The journey of life is long, but we have hung in there together.

- To my parents: Dr. Bruce and Mrs. Debra Jorritsma Prins. Through everything I have experienced over the last 19+ years, you guys have been there to hold my hand and walk beside me. Because of your examples and encouragement, I am here today. I know we have had our fights, disagreements, and hard days, I have still loved you more than anything on earth. There are days where I still wonder why the Father gave me certain things to deal with, and either one of you will always respond with "He's got a plan for you." I thank you for those words, and years we have spent together.

- To my dear friend: Lynnea Sjoerdsma. From the first time I met you, I knew that God had put you in my life for a reason. Coming to terms with God's grace has helped me realize that He put you in my life as a companion on my journey to bring hope to those who need the Father most. Thanks for your encouraging words, your bluntness (at times I needed it), and your hugs. You rock girl!

- To my sister: Julie Nicole Prins. Thanks "Jules" for the lunches in the ADC, the times I used your apartment for rest and getting ready for YULE, for your warm hugs, and for constantly reminding me what love is. Thanks for always saying, "I love you." Those words have made my bad days turn for the better. "Big sister," I could never have asked for someone as special as you to counsel me through some of the hardships of life. Thanks again.

- Lastly, to my father in heaven. I am reminded daily of your love and grace. There are still days when I question why you have given me some of the hardest things to bear, and I am always reassured that you will be there and hold me tight as I take one step at a time toward your open arms of grace and love. Thanks for being the best father. All of us humans have sinned, and still you show love without any end. I am still ready to walk where you lead me, and let you drive that carriage to your destination not mine. Thank you for giving me life and allowing me to have another chance at the journey. I am ever so sorry for my attempts at suicide, as I was trying to end your plan for me, in my time not yours. All I need to do is fall forward into your awaiting arms and I am at peace.

Table of Contents

Forward
Written by Jan Coates[*]

Satan is a liar, but Jesus is truth. Jesus' life and death is the greatest demonstration of truth the world has ever known. That truth is: God loves us— you and me. God did not leave you alone and defenseless in your struggle against Satan. He sent you a champion to fight for you. God's love defeats the deceit Satan uses to enslave us. We need to stand at the foot of His cross. And look up. Through the cross—i.e. the death of Jesus Christ and His resurrection—God completely expresses that He loves all of us. At the cross, God offers us unconditional love and acceptance. And at the cross and the empty tomb, Satan is defeated in your life and mine—forever!

---

[*] Additional texts based on the article Break Free from Shame's Prison and written by Jan Coates. Copyright ©2007, Jan Coates.

"God is love," (1 John 4:8) proclaims the truth of God's character. He created you to love and be loved by Him. Here's something you must know and one of the most important factors I discovered in my love relationship with God: We cannot hide from God. I know. I tried. You may be trying, too. But you cannot escape Him.

Don't try, fall into His arms: today. Now, Just like you are. Surrender: put your hands up and reach for the sky. Feel Satan's chains fall off. Experience a wholehearted, truth-filled, loving relationship with God. Receive unconditional eternal life through Jesus. From the bottom of our hearts, the deepest cavern of our souls, we all yearn for joy and love. No more bondage to the lies of Satan. No more shame. No more guilt. Freedom from the past: Liberty to be all Christ designed us to be.

This is the freedom Jesus offers. This is the truth that will set you free today.

Soul Thoughts

He is able, more than able to accomplish what is hard for me to do today! He is the Alpha, the Warden, the great Attorney, but above all: the Great I Am.

Prologue

Each of us has been trapped in one of earth's prisons at one time or another. Maybe it was something simple like an addiction to chocolate bars or something as large as homosexuality or thoughts of suicide. In each of these situations, we tend to find ourselves separated from God and his idea of us. In the words of Corrie ten Boom: " There is no pit too deep that the love of Jesus is not deeper still." Corrie understood what it meant to be trapped in an earthly prison (physically), but allowed the love of God to triumph and ultimately surrendered the sadness in her heart to the "King of creation."

"The thief comes only to steal and kill and destroy..." (John 10:10a). Nightmares, insomnia, self-hatred, the inability to love or be loved, a lack of trust, depression, self-destructive behaviors, eating disorders, aggressiveness, rage: the list of destruction to the inner depths of the soul goes on and on. Like fallout from a dirty bomb, life experiences can—and will—contaminate nearly every aspect of your life. I know, as an abused child, Satan deceived me. "God can't love YOU," he taunted. "You are unlovable. Dirty. Dirty. Dirty." He penetrated my mind with shame-filled lies. But I have good news. I *experienced* good news: God chooses the most improbable—you and me—to rescue and transform. His truth can set us free from Satan's lies.

When it comes to encroachment by the Devil, all of us deal with it. The Devil's power is strong, but the power of Jesus is ever stronger. He knows what is best for you, and that includes rescuing you from the darkest depths of sin and pain (emotional, physical, and mental). A quadriplegic friend of mine named Renee Bondi wrote these words more than 20-years ago, they go like this:

> Why should I worry, why should I fret. I have a mansion builder who ain't through with me yet. Why should I worry, why should I fret. I have a mansion builder, who ain't through with me yet.

Over the years I have come to realize that no matter how the hard the situation is, or how hard it is to break free from the prison walls, God is more than able to accomplish all things for "he is the master creator, the great I am." In the last decade the God of mercy has set me free from the prisons that controlled every aspect of my life and has made me into the person I am meant to be. The words in this book are words from my heart: they describe my story of freedom from the pits of hell, debauchery, sexual abuse, and suicide. As I walk you through my life's story, I pray you can relate to some of the things I tell you and you may find that there is hope to be rescued from a life of prison hood, guilt, shame, and pain.

Soul Thoughts

*Hell is real, not a mindset or idea from our imagination.
It's a place of imprisonment, of sin, shame, and guilt.
A land of fire where only God is able to penetrate:
He loves each one of us so tenderly that He gave no
second thought when He sent his son to die to save
us from eternal damnation & prison hood!*

In the Midst of Hell

Sitting in that prison, I realized that maybe the Father of grace had a plan. I never knew that attempting suicide would be part of God's purpose for my life. I always thought that people who committed suicide were "dumb-nuts," people who had lost their minds and were satanic of sorts. "How could it have happened to me," I thought as I lay in that cold damp room, on a lumpy mattress, in a semi-furnished room of the psychiatric ward in the Redlands Community Hospital. Trying suicide truly changed my perspective on life and how many teens and young adults feel about the situations of their lives. Life is a precious thing and I now know that. For many, it can take a short snippet with death to realize that or it may take a lifetime, but in any situation, life needs to be lived as though today were your last. The prisons each of us maybe trapped in will not provide the means nor the source for finding peace and understanding who we truly are, they can, however, help you to discover that we have a God who cares enough to say: "My child, greater is thee who is in me, who has chosen to follow me and call me 'Abba Father'."

That lonely room in the psychiatric ward became my friend over the next week as I spent many lonely nights in that room with the door wide open and a nurse sitting in a lounge chair at the door doing crossword puzzles, drinking coffee, or taking a long nap. There were a few nights in that room where I would wake up in tears and I think to myself: "How did I get here, why am I imprisoned in this place?" Then I would realize that I had allowed myself to fall into the hands of the Devil by committing suicide, had I been in my right mind I would never have tried such a stupid (excuse my French) thing like that. God has given each of us a series of trials to deepen our faith, many times those trials seem so unbearable and we allow ourselves to stray from the Saviour and by doing so find that we have ventured onto a road that leads into a prison (many times so painful, it is unbearable).

Soul Thoughts

He bore our cup on Calvary; He knew no other mission but that which came from His father in Heaven. His mission was redemption of sins; Corrie's mission was saving God's chosen people; our mission is letting go of the prisons that bind us!

The Dictionary, a Prison:
my Saviour & Me

In Merriam-Webster's Dictionary, a prison is defined as a state of confinement or captivity; or a place of confinement especially for lawbreakers; *specifically*: an institution (as one under state jurisdiction) for confinement of persons convicted of serious crimes.

One such example occurred in the lives of the ten Boom family: Casper, Betsie, Nollie, Willem, and Corrie. Although they were doing God's will by saving "His chosen people" from the vicious grip of the Nazis, they unlawfully were hiding Jews in a "secret room" carved out of the coat closet in Corrie's upstairs bedroom. Below is a short snippet of how they ended up in the horrific, German concentration camp known as Ravensbrück:

The Germans arrested the entire Ten Boom family on February 28, 1944 at around 12:30 with the help of a Dutch informant. They were first sent to Scheveningen prison (where her father died ten days after his capture). Corrie's sister Nollie, brother Willem, and nephew Peter were all released. Later, Corrie and Betsie were sent to the Vught political concentration camp (both in the Netherlands), and finally to the notorious Ravensbrück concentration camp in Germany on December 16, 1944, where Corrie's sister Betsie died. Before she died she told Corrie, "There is no pit so deep that God's love is not deeper still."

Just like the psychiatric ward held me prisoner, the concentration camp kept Betsie and Corrie chained within its walls. When life seemed at its last, that is when God intervened in the situation and allowed Corrie and Betsie to be people for him, even in the midst of a place filled with darkness. God can take the most horrid situations and use them as jewels in his kingdom: transforming those willing to persevere in the middle of hardship. Just as he chose Ravensbrück as a place for Christ's love to abound, he uses psychiatric wards all over the world to make an impact on lives of people suffering from the idea that darkness and prison hood is their only friend.

Although this maybe the popular, well-known definition for the term prison, the Bible defines the word in a different way: in a general sense, any place of confinement or involuntary restraint; but appropriately, a public building for the confinement or safe custody of debtors and criminals committed by process of law; a jail. Originally, a prison, as Lord Coke observes, was only a place of safe custody; but it is now employed as a place of punishment. We have state prisons, for the confinement of criminals by way of punishment. The book of Ecclesiastes defines prison as a low, obscure, afflicted condition (Ecclesiastes 4, NIV, 1982). While Isaiah defines being in prison as a state of spiritual bondage (Isaiah 42, NIV, 1982). In a sense, we are all in a state of spiritual bondage at sometime in our sinful lives. Because we are sinful, a cage of wickedness surrounds us and bans us from being in communion with God the Father. Spiritual bondage can only be broken when we come to terms with the idea that we are not able to live life in our present state, and, therefore, require the help of God to follow the road laid before us. To some extent, Jesus (although perfect) felt a sense of spiritual bondage as he prayed in the

Garden of Gethsemane. He was struggling with the idea that he would have to get on an old rugged cross and bear the sins of all the world; he wondered why someone as perfect as himself would have to do that. But in the end he allowed himself to say these words: "Father take this cup from me, only if it be "**your will**." If not, I will let "**your will**" be done" (paraphrase of Matthew 26:39, NIV, 1982). Not only did Jesus suffer from a spiritual prison, he was imprisoned physically. He was torn and beaten, flogged and stabbed with spears; was nailed to a tree and laid in a rock. But the Saviour never once backed from His mission; he followed the "**will of his Father**," and was imprisoned by the sins of this world. As the Christ hung on that cross, His father turned his back on him. For the God of Abraham, Isaac, and Jacob could not bear to see our sins. In the same way, He cannot bear to see us in prisons of doom and, many times Hell, so he willingly frees us and gives redemption.

Soul Thoughts

*This is my blood of the covenant, which is poured
out for many for the forgiveness of sins.*
-----------------Matthew 26:28

Could there be Such a Thing as Forgiveness and Freedom?

Jesus' experiences relate to ours in many ways: after all, he took on human form and acted just like a human would. However, he acted in perfection, he bore a cross without complaint, while we are asked to bear crosses and grudgingly try to fulfill that task. Our crosses come in many forms, just like our prisons. As I continue to share with you more of my story, I pray that you will grasp onto the idea that:

> There is a cross meant for you to carry;
> there is a cross meant for you alone. As you
> bow down in humble surrender: God is the
> strength for your journey.

The first night in that prison I lay in the bed as the lights were turned off. Tears began to form in my eyes as I cried out to the Abba Father: "Father, I know I don't deserve your grace, but forgive me for trying to destroy your perfect creation. Please forgive a wretch like me, Father." I knew that I didn't deserve the grace and mercy that only the mighty God could give, but I asked anyway. Prisons are the worst of things, but maybe even the best of things: they teach you to surrender your imperfections and mistakes to the foot of Christ's cross. For me, committing suicide may have been just that.

I continued crying out to Him until I had no strength left (or so I thought). By the Father's grace I was able to cry out one last time: "Father, let me out of this prison; let me out of this pit of Hell." I honestly don't know how, but in the blink of an eye, I physically saw the walls of that prison come crashing down, as Christ was victorious once again. With one mighty blow, those walls were no more and I stood face to face with my "Abba Father." At that point, I realized that I had been imprisoned: physically, mentally, and spiritually. Physically, I was locked away in a psychiatric ward, being controlled by doctors and nurses. On top of that, I was stuck in the land of fire: I could physically see the Devil himself. I realized that physical capture was the most terrifying thing in the whole universe. Locked in the Devil's land with no way out made me rethink how I viewed a gift like life. Mentally, I had built up this notion inside my head that I was worthless, had no idea of who I was, and didn't belong in a world of "perfect" people. In that instance too, I also had some rethinking to do: I had to come to terms with who the God of grace wanted me to be. Spiritually, I was in the grip of Satan. I had been so mentally delusioned that I allowed myself to turn my back on the "true Father" and succumb to the power of the "evil one." In one night, the tables turned and I was receiving forgiveness from the master creator once again.

The imprisonment I have just shared with you is by no means a vacation experience. To put it kindly, "it was Hell on earth." I almost wish that I had never been given the gifts that the Master had given me, but then I wouldn't have the opportunity to share with you this story, and many more, in this book. Hell is not a joyride nor is it a honeymoon vacation: it is death, eternal refuse, and slime and prison hood. As this chapter of my life comes to its end, I realize that prisons are everywhere, and we all get trapped in them some how. Imprisonment is not a bad thing, but merely a God thing as it teaches you to trust that He will be the "wind beneath your wings" and walk you through the hard times.

Soul Thoughts

In a similar way, Sodom and Gomorrah and the surrounding towns gave themselves up to sexual immorality and perversion. They serve as an example of those who suffer the punishment of eternal fire.

------------------Jude 1:7

Sexuality: Who are We Really?

Realizing your identity is a big thing these days. Are you a man, a woman, have you changed sexes: who are you. For me this begins the next chapter of this book. As I tell you about additional personal events of my life I pray that God shines new light on each of your situations and helps set you free from your prison.

You would never have guessed that I had been a victim of a sex predator, nor the perpetrator of debauchery, nor envisioned the idea of homosexuality, but I did. Christmas time is supposed to be a family affair: turkey dinners, pumpkin pie, Christmas cookies, apple cider, parties, finger foods, the whole enchilada, but in my mind something else was stirring: the idea of becoming homosexual. These thoughts seemed weird to me as all my life I knew that homosexuality was morally and Biblically wrong, but I couldn't help myself get over the idea.

Many times prisons go from one thing to the next: they can take on multiple forms at multiple times. In my case, the prison went from suicide to debauchery and then homosexuality. It wasn't like I wanted to be thinking about the horrid topic, it just seemed to come. I thought that there was no way around it and I became trapped in a place that was new and very frightening to me. But, like in all situations, God had a plan and he planned to use this downfall of mine to help me trust in him even more.

Is There a Place for Another Bout of Forgiveness?

What started out as curiosity began to turn into a realization. The things I thought about were constantly focused on homosexuality and debauchery. Life can turn so drastically in a very short time: what once seemed wrong, becomes a common thing.

As my addiction to the thoughts became more real, I found myself imprisoned by the sin being committed. Finding myself in darkness, I seemed to neglect the idea that there was hope and victory over my sin. The chains of sin (from both my past and present) had taken me and bound me to a tree stuck in the middle of a river of despair. As the weeks went on, I became the victim of a sex predator.

Apparently, this person had sent me a message through facebook that went something like this:

> How are you? My name is so and so. I am
> 20-years old and live in West Hollywood,
> California. I would like to meet you and find
> out more about you and your family.

At the time, I paid no attention to the message and deleted it. Next thing I know I am receiving text messages from this unknown person saying things like:

> I'm going to put my penis up your butt. Let's
> go have fun and play in the shower. Why
> don't we strip and sleep together.

Not only did I receive profane messages, but also I began getting sexually oriented pictures of the guy in the nude. I don't know how I got involved, but I did. In a sense I was a prisoner to an unknown sex predator. I was tricked into going along with his game and began texting him similar pictures and speaking his language of ungodliness.

There are times when individuals with alternative motifs grab us all. I was made into an object of sex for a gay man who thought that it would be fun to take an innocent young person and use them for pleasurable things. Not only did I make a poor choice by following this guy's wishes, I also damaged a lifestyle of redemption that I was living: but that experience strengthened my faith in the "Abba Father" and I learned to trust him more. Homosexuality, and even debauchery, is not the God-given lifestyle you want to live, God created each of us to live lives of purity and surrender, to commune with Him. When we choose to practice something as horrid as debauchery, we have made a choice to break that union we have with Christ; we are also making ourselves vulnerable to the will of the Devil and are refusing the plan of a lifelong commitment: one man+one woman = marriage.

Soul Thoughts

And the angels who did not keep their positions of authority but abandoned their own home—these he has kept in darkness, bound with everlasting chains for judgment on the great Day.

-----------------Jude 1:6

Chains That Held Tight

The sin that I had committed held on tight for several months. I felt like no matter where I went the I was the prisoner of something as horrid as debauchery and homosexuality. The chains that shackled me were unbearable, but every time I tried to get myself out of the prison I dug myself a deeper pit of sin. One little sin can have the worst effects on a person: spiritual deprivation, mental captivity, and physical sorrow. The God of grace could only break the chains of this prison, but how could I face him when I had nearly taken my life before, and now this. When we are in situations like this, the Holy Spirit acts as an attorney of sorts that brings our case before the Judge (God the Father), and our attorney defends us so that we can be let go from prison (being released seems like a dream come true, but consequences for our sins are also required).

It was a God thing when the sin of debauchery was revealed as I knew that by keeping it a secret it was only hindering my growth as I tried to move on with my life. When that sin came out, I could sense that the chains binding me had been released and I was able to stand face to face with my Father in Heaven and ask for the needed forgiveness. Debauchery and homosexuality, in any form, are lifestyles and ideas that should not be taken lightly. They can enchain you for decades, leaving you trying to live multiple lives as you try to fit in and be human. These two prisons can cause even more pain, shame, and guilt to arise than the original problem. When the problem gets bigger, the burden becomes harder to bear and the victim finds him/herself in a deeper pit than before and the prison walls become harder to see over. The Apostle Luke spoke these words:

> For we do not have a High Priest who is unable to sympathize with our weaknesses, but we have one who has been tempted in every way, just as we are—yet was without sin (Hebrews 4:15, NIV, 1982).

Christ bore our pain, guilt, and shame on a cross: He too was tempted with the things of this world, but He refused to let them influence the "**will of His Father in Heaven**." We in the same way can break free from earthly prisons and be released from the pits of Hell when we trust in the Father to help us be victors. We then need to acknowledge our downfalls and allow God to change us into the person He intends us to be: we are not perfect, we are tempted by the evils of this world, but we are victors over Hell because of a Saviour.

The chains that held me tight were broken by Christ's victory on the cross. He shed his blood for you and me. He acknowledged that we were sinful but went through with the sacrifice anyway. I realized that I could not live a life tormented by debauchery and turned the wickedness in my life over to the redeemer and ultimate judge. He crushed my sins into a pulp, and forgave and forgot. My sin is no more and I am free of all the darkness that plagued my life.

The shame that came as a result of my actions still plagues me, but I can claim freedom. Freedom from prison is not merely physical, but spiritual, mental, and emotional. In my case, once the chains of darkness were crushed by Christ's mighty blow, I became an ex-convict, a prisoner of the past. I received grace beyond measure, and by His grace alone I overcame all things of the world. Physically

I am still bound by the consequences of my actions, but spiritually I am renewed in the presence of my Father: Oh how he loves you and me, He gave his life what more could he give, Oh how he loves you and me. Realizing that no matter the greatness of your sin, He gave his life because He so tenderly cares for you.

Soul Thoughts

A looking glass is for looking; a glass ball is for predicting the future; but Christ is everlasting: look to Him for guidance and He reveals the things you need most!

Looking Through a Glass Ball

Imagine being the black sheep in a group of people, the lone ranger of sorts, the outsider, and the misfit. Believe me, I was all of that and more growing up. As I take you through another part of my journey to freedom I pray that you see once again that prisons can be anything from physical prison like a psychiatric ward to spiritual and moral prisons like homosexuality to mental and social prisons like living with Asperger Syndrome: a type of autism. Asperger patients often show various abnormalities in bahaviour, but these are usually outnumbered by their strengths: people person, mature beyond age, and intellectual advantage. The following are symptoms (some common, some less) of people with AS:

- Asperger Syndrome is an autism spectrum disorder, and people with it therefore show significant difficulties in social interaction, along with restricted and repetitive patterns of behavior and interests. It differs from other autism spectrum disorders by its relative preservation of linguistic and cognitive development. Although not required for diagnosis, physical clumsiness and atypical use of language are frequently reported. Symptoms of this disorder include:

- Most people with Asperger's Syndrome are of average or above average intelligence.

- They have excellent thinking skills where things are concerned but are extremely poor at interpreting human relationships.

- Intense preoccupations often centre on certain toys or areas of interest. Common obsessions are dinosaurs and forms of transport and how they work.

- They will often seek out other people to talk to about their interests. The conversation is usually one-sided – more like a lecture where they talk about their knowledge and aren't interested in feedback.

- Older children may enjoy a club that is focused on their interest – for example, coin or stamp collecting.

- Eye contact is not understood or made use of.

- The child may appear cold and uncaring but it is not deliberate. He does not think about others and cannot understand the social graces that keep society functioning.

- It is possible to teach social skills but it is a long slow process and often requires parental intervention to repair social damage when they act inappropriately.

- Short stories can be useful in teaching social skills. Use one page visual aids that teach about listening to others and keeping quiet and still while they talk.

- Children with Asperger's Syndrome prefer routine and structure and can become irritable and distressed if the unexpected happens.

- Gross and fine motor skills are often underdeveloped, causing problems in sports and balance.

- Asperger's Syndrome is often detected when a child starts preschool. He will generally interact better with his teacher than his peers and may display silly, loud, aggressive or socially withdrawn behaviour.

- Things are interpreted very literally, meaning that sarcasm, playful teasing and figures of speech are not understood.

- Rules are very important and a child may become angry if a game is not played fairly or his peers break school rules.

- On a positive note, this aversion to rule-breaking means the Asperger's Syndrome child is less likely to experiment with smoking, drinking, drugs, and sex as he matures.

- Many children are perfectionists and struggle if they fail to produce perfect schoolwork. Encourage them to move on, and create distractions if necessary to get them to continue working.

- They find it hard to generalize. If taught that they shouldn't hit a child at school, they do not automatically make the connection that they shouldn't hit a child in the mall.

- Children with Asperger's Syndrome express their feelings in unpredictable ways. Sometimes they may seem emotionless and other times they may display extreme emotion that is not appropriate to the situation.

- Interrupting conversations is a common problem as the child does not understand the social signals that allow conversation to move from one to another.

- A child can be helped if parents consistently work with him and highlight his strengths and work consistently on his weaknesses.

Autism is a disorder of neural development characterized by impaired social interaction and communication, and by restricted and repetitive behavior. These signs all begin before a child is three years old. Autism affects information processing in the brain by altering how nerve cells and their synapses connect and organize; how this occurs is not well understood.

I grew up in my own special world, I could say. I had no real friends, I was intelligent beyond my years, acted differently, talked with the "mature" adults most of my life, yet I never knew what it meant to have friends of my own. I was encapsulated by this world of differentness: I didn't know why the other people didn't want to treat me like a normal person, I didn't know what I had done wrong to make them want to leave or come one minute and the next be gone. To me, I was just being myself. I was acting like, what I perceived as, any other child would. However, as I got older, I soon discovered that life is more about peer relationships and less about myself (including my own little world).

I first discovered that I was different when I was elementary school. Like most normal kids, I was expected to make friends with kids my own age by the time I was in kindergarten. But instead, all my friends remained the adults: in this case the teachers. I would spend almost every afternoon in the principal's office talking and eating cookies with the her. We became good friends (and still, after almost 14 years, talk and keep in touch) and most of my early childhood memories were spent in either a teacher's classroom or the principal's office. If a diagnosis had been made sooner, maybe I would not have had to deal with the loneliness that comes from Asperger Syndrome.

The capsule of my life was slowly getting smaller as time went by. I was learning things about myself that I had not noticed before. I began to realize that I was different but had no way to be like everybody else. I was chained to the idea that I was a freak, I had no one who understood me or who I was: I was the nerd. I had problems with friends all throughout middle school, high school and the beginning of my college career; I had boundary issues, said things that were true but hurtful, acted in ways that I thought were normal, and did things to my own life that I now regret. I had no clue that life could be so different than what it was, I had thought that the actions of others were the ones affecting me and not vice versa. But out of my own encapsulation, I was affecting the lives of others through my actions: I ruined relationships, harmed the mentality of others, and down right messed up. I only wish that I could have been normal. I wished I was normal, I wanted to have friends, and I wanted people to treat me like me and not run away and hide every time they saw me.

Normality can have a variety of meanings or connotations. In my case, normal was being accepted, looking and acting like everyone else, feelings like I actually belonged: feeling encaged made me feel separated far greater than epilepsy ever had. Feeling different had its challenges: could I ever be the person God created me to be; would I ever succeed; was I able to have a relationship with someone. But in the midst of all my pain and loneliness, the God of grace had the ball moving and was using this roadblock to get me closer to others with disabilities.

Try being the geek of the crowd and never knowing you have something known as Asperger's; try reaching your arm out to give someone a hug and then that same person screams and calls you names because they think you are trying to do something inappropriate to them. There were times when I thought it was okay to go up to a girl and touch her hair, give her a big hug and call her sweetie or some other name of affection. That incident usually ended with the girl walking away with a snooty look on her face that meant: "What do you think you are doing?" Looking back, I realize that my actions were, in a sense, out of my control: it was something that came with my imprisonment by Asperger's Syndrome and something that I thought was expected by society. The things that seem hard for me are actually very easy for others to learn and do: because of my socially unstable lifestyle, I am constantly having to relearn the simplest things and have spent many nights in tears as I try to uncover the mystery of me, and who God really made me to be.

Imprisonment by a disease, such as: AS, is by no means easy. It took nearly 16-years of loneliness, being a black sheep of society (and my family), and wandering in darkness. When a diagnosis came in April of 2009, I was let free from my social prison: I could finally understand my situation and how to begin fixing it. Fixing the past is not such an easy thing, especially when mistakes were made without a reasonable cause. Challenges of a social disorder are never enjoyable, but they are building blocks of our relationship with God. God will only give us as much as He thinks we can handle, nothing more and nothing less. When He thinks we can't do it, He holds our hand and walks us through the journey. God is truly a loving God; no one knows about our social, mental, emotional, and physical make up like he does. AS causes a "you fix it" momentum to be infixed within us. We learn to rebuild relationships, slowly develop verbal filters, relearn the idea of boundaries, and begin the process (once again) of earning the trust of those we have hurt. I pray God uses your challenges as stepping-stones in your faith and draws you nearer to the "Abba Father." In Hebrews 4:15 it says: "For we do not have a High Priest who is unable to sympathize with our weaknesses, but we have one who has been tempted in every way, just as we are—yet was without sin" (Hebrews 4:15, NIV, 1982). This book has brought me much comfort and peace as I have shared my heart, a tidbit of my life's story, and most of all shared the story of my Saviour and me as we have walked this journey together.

The following three chapters contain additional thoughts from my heart: thoughts that truly help the reader of this book understand that we have a God who is good, one who is all powerful, and one who so tenderly cares for each of us. He is a God of righteousness and because of His grace all of our mistakes and the walls of our prisons are no more. If you are struggling and stuck in a prison, please don't hesitate to go to my website (georgenewmanministries.org) and find additional information on how to find freedom in Jesus Christ and return to the path he created just for you. Remember! There is a Saviour, a Master Creator. Each time we come into His presence, we stand in wonder once again. His grace is still amazing, and what a great thing it is to know we have a Father who cares enough to say: "My child, greater is thee who comes to me carrying weakness and burden. For I will make thee a warrior of Christ." Though the road, on this journey called life, may be hard and steep and filled with pain: God is ever present. He holds our hand and guides us along the road created just for you and me. God is too wise to be mistaken. God is too good to be unkind. So when you don't understand; you can't see His plan; you can't trace His hand; trust His heart.

In the Father's Hands

There is no pit to deep, that the love of Jesus isn't deeper still!

As life goes on we experience more pain. Pain teaches us to rely on Him, Him who gives us everlasting strength and peace. God's peace is often defined as spiritual quietness given to those who are emotionally, spiritually, or physically struggling. This peace has brought many people into the loving arms of Jesus because only through Him are we at rest.

Over the years, I think about the hardships I have gone through. I realize that if the Lord Jesus had not allowed these painful things to happen, many people may not know the saving grace of Him. I remember wanting to give up on life because I could not handle what was going on around me. Through these dark times, I found eternal peace in my "Abba" Father. He cares for us like a shepherd cares for his sheep. He knows what you are going through (Hebrews 4:15-16 KJV), so come to him with your hurting heart and your needs: for the Lord Jesus is always there. Corrie ten Boom once said,

"If His will be your will, and your way be His way, then all of your insufficiency and inaptitude shall be met by the sufficiency of His grace. Obey the voice of the Lord Jesus, who says, 'Come unto me, all ye that labor and are heavy laden, and I shall give you rest' (Matthew 11:28 KJV). Come! Like a mother says to a fearful child, 'Come.' Nothing else is necessary. When you come to Him, He does the job."

Many times we reject the place that our Heavenly Father has for us in Heaven. This is our choice, because the tempter is causing us to deny Christ. We must overcome this sin and constantly ask the Lord for help. Jesus says, "Behold! I stand at the door and knock: if any man shall hear my voice, and then open the door, I will come in..." (Revelation 3:20 KJV). Though we deny the Lord, He constantly says come. We need the Almighty Father, because without him we are sinful. We can rejoice that He has cleansed us from all unrighteousness because of His sacrifice on Calvary. Shall we not surrender to Him who can make us His victorious artists? Yes, we can; but only through His help can we find strength and guidance to carry on through the hardships of life.

I pray that you will find strength and comfort. My struggles have been allowed so that I might be a light for the Savior, and I might tramp for His everlasting glory. Find peace in the Lord, for He cares for you and shall give you strength.

Soul Thoughts

Will you choose to believe that you are beautiful? Will you be the one to say: "I am loved by my creator, for I am made in His perfect image?" Will you be the one?

God's Image

What the world thinks of you is hogwash; what Jesus thinks of you is what really counts!

Prepare yourself to be filled with the everlasting peace of Jesus. His peace can fill our darkest wounds with gladness, and cleanse our souls from faithlessness. Christ has conquered more than earthly death when He died on Calvary; He conquered the Devil's hold on our lives. No longer are we trapped by the pain and suffering the world brings, but we can rejoice in that suffering as if it were a "ticker tape parade" celebrating an accomplishment in our lives. God does not want us to succumb to the things of this earth, but as humans, born of a sinful nature, we are accustomed to such things. God has a better plan for us, just as He did for me. He has transformed me into messenger for his name, to bring others into His bosom of never ending love. He wants us to come into that bosom as if we were helpless infants needing our mother's protection. God does not want us to come to Him only in times of distress; we have a Father who wants us to approach the "throne of grace" even when we have been found guilty. He shows us his mercy and cleanses us from within, making us more in his image. This is a process that continues throughout life as we come to realize how precious we are to the father, how His grace is greater than anyone of our sins.

After attempting suicide in January of this year, I was sent to the psychiatric ward of the local community hospital and remained in its clutches for nearly a week. Being in that hospital was both a rewarding experience and signs of downfall on my part. I was able to not only minister to the other inhabitants, but also to gain knowledge about how to deal with life's turmoil and topsy-turvy roads. But on the other hand, I felt like I was in a steel prison cell with no way out. I could not just go up to a nurse and request to be released because I was placed on 51-50, in this case endangerment to one's self, but I truly was being clutched in the fiery hands of the Devil. The Devil saw me as a prime target, not only because I appeared helpless but also because I was in a state of functioning where I felt the Father had deserted me. Through some divine intervention, I was able to cry out to my "Abba" Father and be released from the pits of hell. I was able to cry out for forgiveness and mercy, and was ultimately given a new start on life. Although I recovered from this ordeal rather quickly, I still had much to learn about my image and God's idea of it. God did not want me to try and fit in with the world around me (look where it got me last time), He wanted me to be me, nothing more. His view of my person was from the inside while mine was from the outside. He views me as a beautiful creation while I don't have the mental capacity to envision such things, but with his help I can become confident and no longer feel worthless or ashamed.

Soul Thoughts

The Devil is a liar. He tampers with our minds: your mind is one of your most precious gifts from God, once gone you can no longer get it or its thoughts back! Trust God to be your shield against all of the Devil's temptations and ask Him to guard your heart and mind.

The Battle for the Mind

Shame is one of Satan's weapons to keep you hiding from God. Make no mistake: Shame is not the same as guilt. Guilt stems from our own wrong actions. Shame—warranted or unwarranted—is humiliation we are taught. We perpetuate shame by treating ourselves as unworthy of forgiveness. Shame can be the penetrating tip of a lie shot at us by Satan. The real lie Satan wants us to believe is that we are too guilty to be forgiven and accepted by God. Jesus died to tell us the opposite, but Satan will pierce us so deeply with his lie that we may not be able to comprehend the truth. Over and over, Satan will whisper, "You're no good. Don't even think about talking to God because He won't give someone like you the time of day." Beware, friends: Words like these create an evil trap rigged with chains for your soul. By paralyzing you with anguish, Satan will deceive you into thinking you are unworthy of God's love. Satan will trap you in a prison of misery as he devours your soul, sucking your life dry of all joy in the process.

I really don't want to give the Evil One much space: yet sometimes, we need to remember he truly does exist. Scripture reveals his existence as a spirit of evil from Genesis to Revelation. God threw Satan out of heaven because of his wicked ways. His names include: serpent, accuser, dragon, and enemy, man of sin, power of darkness, devourer, devil, and tempter. These names clearly describe his dark character. Jesus called Satan "...the father of lies."

Like it or not, Satan is real. Satan desires to destroy the lives—yours and mine—by sin. He ambushes us with half-truths, deceit, and outright lies. He uses past experiences to plant thoughts that make us feel, hopeless, rejected, and defeated. By these, Satan deceives us into believing we are not worthy to seek Jesus. He will not rest until he robs us of our worth, future, and very souls.

So what's our defense against him? When we call out to God in surrender, He rescues us. Our confidence in Him is based on the rock-solid promises of God—the truth.

Epilogue

Writing this memoir/biography has been a dream come true. I waited quite a while to sit down and pen words from my heart: words that only God can give. I had a choice when writing these words. I could either listen to God saying: "Harrison you can write these words on your own, trusting I will give them to you"; I could also ignore Him and then have Him say: "Harrison I am going to kick you in the pants and make you do it. Either way you have to share your story with those who need it most." When God says those words, it means we had better do it: never estimate the power of God. My life is not perfect, I have seen both sides of life: Hell and Heaven. I spent a good 5+ hours in the glories of Heaven back in January of 2009, and spent a similar amount of time, if not more, in Hell three days later.

Each of us bears some hardship and unless it is taken to the foot of Christ's cross we end up imprisoned by our imperfections and sin. I may not have all the answers when it comes to being released from the worst of all places, but I do have a lifetime spent walking with my Jesus. Jesus has walked by my side from day one carrying me through one prison after another: I have ventured probably as far away from God as any human can go but He allowed me the opportunity to reconcile myself before the throne of Grace.

A friend of mine recently recorded a popular Christian song with her college choir. The lyrics to the song go:

> Like a newborn baby don't be afraid to crawl
> and remember when you walk you're going
> to fall: so fall on Jesus, fall on Jesus and live.
> When the love spills over and music fills the
> night and when you can't contain the joy
> inside: dance for Jesus, dance for Jesus and
> live.

Those lyrics hold a special place in my heart as they have helped my walk with Christ. When I fall, I am going to fall on Jesus; when I dance, then I am going to dance with all my heart for my Jesus. He is the Saviour and he cares for each soul making all hearts whole. He loved each of us enough to say: "Yes Father I will take their place on Calvary and die. I will be the sacrificial lamb for their sake." God the Father knew that my sins were never going to allow me to see him face to face and allow me the opportunity to stand before him and receive grace a multitude of times, but He sent Jesus to die on Calvary and that was sufficient payment. Christ's victory is one example of freedom from imprisonment; others include: being found innocent of charges against you, finding out the diagnosis of a disease, and seeking psychological help for a mental disorder. Even though we all suffer in a prison, there is hope. Hope causes perseverance to develop, and perseverance causes trust in the "Father of grace" to abound.